When Silence Speaks And The Mind Whispers........

Profound rumination....

Karan Sood

Made with ❤ on the BookLeaf Publishing Platform
www.bookleafpub.in
www.bookleafpub.com

Dedication

Poetry begins where words fail. It lingers....

To my family, who gave me roots, and to the quiet moments that became verses.

To you- The one holding this book.

Preface

Poetry, for me, has always been a quiet place—a place to feel, to question, to unravel, and to begin again. This collection was born from moments both tender and tumultuous, from silence and noise, from love, loss, longing, and everything in between.

These poems are on the moments close to my heart, and when I say close to my heart I refer to the moments that have touched me at some point of life. After completing my work I have always wondered whether this has been penned by me…..the words just come with a flow and writing has always taken me to a different world where I am not myself. That's the beauty of imagination and creativity I believe.

Each poem is a fragment of experience, a reflection of a moment I needed to capture before it slipped away. Some came in a rush, urgent and unfiltered. Others arrived slowly, whispering themselves into being. Together, they form a tapestry of my inner world—a landscape of emotion, memory, and imagination.

A journey through this unique work will help you decipher that it is motivated from simple instances which have happened with me and made me brood over. It's about common life incidents which very few people pay heed to or even if they do, they don't have the acceptance for the same. I believe my poems portray the events as seen through the eyes of the mind. Usually aimlessly wandering thoughts do find some destination.

Hope this book with unique poetry captivates your emotions, thoughts and imagination with every read. If even a single poem of the collections makes you think for a moment it would be rewarding.

This book with unique poetry isn't meant to offer answers. Rather, it's an invitation—to feel deeply, to pause, to reflect. If even one line stays with you, or makes you think for a moment, then this collection has done its work.

Thank you for stepping into these pages.

— Karan

Acknowledgements

This collection would not exist without the love, support, and inspiration that have surrounded me on this journey. To the muses—both seen and unseen—who whispered verses into my thoughts and stirred emotions into ink, thank you.

To my family and friends, for encouraging every word, for believing in my voice even when I doubted it—your support means more than words can say.

To the poets who came before me, whose work lit the path and showed me what is possible with language, thank you for teaching me the power of vulnerability.

To BookLeaf Publishing, the opportunity you offered has brought this book to life. I am deeply grateful for your presence along the way.

And to you, dear reader—thank you for opening these pages and walking through this world of words with me. May you find something here that resonates, lingers, and maybe even heals.

--- Karan

1. "Intent of Burning to Generosity"

In a dark silent night I was in study and reading,
All of a sudden light went off and my foot was leading.
I began to search for the candle to lighten the place,
It was somewhat like a transition phase.

As I lit the candle I wondered what a glory,
The candle with a wick in it is a good story.
The wax is a protection and gives wick a support
The wick burns itself to light no matter how hot.

I could hear the wick say, "I burn myself for the
ambience that surrounds,
I bear the pain of burning shortening my life to be
around.
But then this is for what I am made, burning is my fate,
I die burning, burning and burning no matter how late."

As I stood there adoring the wick and its passion,
A sharpened pencil on the table caught my attention.

The pencil lead that was peeping out seem to say
"I have a similar fate; for service this is how I pay,
I bear the pain of sharpening knowing my life would
end,
This is what I do, 'To keep writing and come to an end'".

Cool breeze from the window shook the wick and it
swayed
It withstood the breeze and firm like a mountain stayed.
I glimpsed at the candle wick which still burnt bright,
Smilingly I turned to the pencil as if to say, "See what a
plight?"

Standing there I wondered why? Why am I in such a
situation?
What have I to do with this candle and pencil equation?
Just then I thought to pay circumstances a heed,
To understand the hidden message is the need.

In this fleeting time, as the candle's flame flickers bright,
And the pencil wears down, both losing their fight.
Though their bodies may shorten, their purpose is clear,
In service to others, they conquer their fear

Wick lightens the places; writings from lead enlighten
the minds,

Both are unique and serve in as their own respective
kinds.
Let us as humans cultivate such thoughts.
In the worldly desires lets not be caught.

So let us embrace this cycle of giving,
With each sacrifice made, a richness of living.
For in the act of lighting and crafting a thought,
Lies a legacy of love that cannot be bought.

Together we stand, like the wick and the lead
Creating a warmth, as our spirits are fed
In the quiet of night, may our hearts take a stand
To share our own light, to lend out a hand.

For life is but a candle, burning ever so bright,
A journey of shadows, transforming through light.
So let us not falter, nor shy from our role,
To burn for each other, and heal every soul.

2. "Blissful Night"

Sometimes at night, while gazing at sky,
I wonder and ask myself why?
Why do the stars that shine so bright,
Loose their identity in broad daylight?

The question unanswered makes me brood,
And I here by try to conclude.

In darkness of night stars shine and glow,
Adding to the beauty and make romance flow.
Dark, silent night and serene atmosphere,
Spellbound you with the beauty which is there.

I thought of the lovers, who talk of moon,
Will they ever talk about it at noon?
The beauty of moon in the dark with stars around,
Is the connection (apart from heart) which Love has
found.

When the starry sky lightens up the hearts,

That's where and when the Love starts.
Two body one soul separated by distance and no matter
how far,
Feel each others presence in the beauty of moon and star.

Such re-union of hearts through the jewels of sky,
Such moments with spirits all time high
Such a solace when your love is not close,
In the dark glory of night with twinkling stars is what
God chose.

That's why the embellished sky walks away,
For the sweet memories to stay throughout the day.
As day elapses with the wait for the beautiful night,
The star-studded sky flaunts with all its might.

I again start gazing at stars in the sky,
I wonder and ask myself why?
Why this thought even crossed my mind?
When day light can't offer this and night is so kind.

3. "A Known Yet Unknown Experience"

As I was standing in front of my window on a cold winte
r day
I wondered why? Why is it so cold today?

Since my childhood I had seen this view, though nothing
was new,
But still there was something in it which held me there li
ke glue
Mesmerized was I to see the pigeons that flew in the sky,
As I followed them through, they took me to the mounta
ins high.

The mountains in all their beauty, stood firm and exotic,
High Hills with sparkling lights, the view made me franti
c.
Embellished with stars, the mountains gave a panoramic
view,
I started wondering what is this all for and how is this ne
w?

The White fog smeared all over and it seemed that the st
ars that shone so bright,
Were fighting for existence with the fog and slowly got l
ost in broad day light
Slow moment of fog gave the mountain a new look of a
white floating sheet,
As fog moved over the mountains, it appeared that the cl
ouds have descended to meet.

I moved my eyes back in the vicinity of the window in a
very awkward fashion,
Just then a newly renovated house at a stone's throw cau
ght my attention.
"Renovation" this was what was the whole scenario's int
ention.
Acceptance of "Change is the law of nature" is worth a m
ention.

It was not the day's cold that made me brood,
It was a hidden message which was to be understood.
Just as the old house was demolished and got renovated i
n color snow white,
Similarly the fog renovated the lighted mountains to eng
ulf the starry sight.

Just then I felt the breeze and the freezing cold on my ha
nds and nose,
I realized relationship between nature and human life is s
o close.

As I pondered the whispers of winter's frozen breath,
I felt the heartbeat of seasons, entwined in life and death
Each gust carried stories of warmth buried deep,
Reminding me softly of promises we keep.

So here at my window, on this cold winter's day,
I cling to the lesson the frost has to say.
For in every chill, in every fleeting moment's grace,
Lies the beauty of living, the warmth of embrace.

4. "Blessed Child"

A sitting lonely child caught my attention,
Something drew me to her in all compassion.
Didn't know a surprise awaited me as I will get near,
Shocked was I to see she could neither see nor hear.
Sitting there all by herself singing her tunes,
She had no interest in Looney tunes.
She had no idea what the world looks like,
She had no idea what is dark and what is light.

She was what the world calls "disabled"
Blessed with a quality unparalleled
Stunned and mesmerized was I to see,
As I approached her she could sense me.
This made me quiet and I didn't respond to
As she stopped murmuring and asked who?
This innate quality in her was unique
Like a naïve into her world I wanted to sneak

Like an observer I stood there analyzing,
Her acts were more and more surprising.

As another child approached her she called his name,
No sight, no word, no touch still true. Ghosh! What a
game?
He held her hand and made a gesture to move,
She got up and eloped like a princess in her grove.
As she left I watched her and stood there in complete
cogitation,
And wondered why my mind was in a state of agitation?

Why this little incident has impacted me this way?
When daily many such small things come our way.
I am still confused and inconclusive over the fact,
But there was something to learn from this small act.
I am sure through such life's experiences are earned
A wise thought and meaning of life is what I have learnt

I understood not everyone is blessed alike
It's not always that everyone has same spike

Now I am sure not everyone shares same thoughts
To compare, think not all fingers are alike if u spot
Difference of opinion is what always prevails
Not all towards one destination sail
Ironically the things in life you find appealing
For other person the same might not be so revealing

In God's Family all of us have a place

Let the disabled live their life with grace
Do believe they deserve a shot at life
With impairment let not life act as a knife.
"Disabled" people cannot help being this way,
Ooh! That's the most inappropriate word I hate to say.

"Unparalleled" or "beatified" is what I would love to use,
Almighty is the one who this life for them chose
It's our moral responsibility to help them rise
Few appreciating words are what would apprise.
A blessed child has unnoticed skills and million dreams
Let them not fade and go unnoticed in the worlds
screams.

5. "Humming River"

Sitting on a river side as I saw the river flow
I wondered why? Why is it so?
I closed my eyes and could hear it sing a song,
"I have travelled far and will travel long
I never get tired I never stop flowing
It's my life and this is how it's going,
Flowing from the mountains and through the hills
Life and beauty into my surroundings I fill.
Downstream towards my destination I flow
Oceans wait for me with wide open arms and a glow.
On my way down many I meet, many I see,
Aha many here have fallen for me (love me),
Needless to mention my two banks are my passion,
Both are love of my life and steady devotion.
They walk side by side; they walk hand in hand,
They are with me no matter what type of land.
They have seen me smiling they have seen me weep,
They have always been with me in every leap.
At times when I am restless and get infuriated
At such testing times my banks are fully merited

They are my inseparable mates and always beside,
Loving them is what I can never hide.
Oneness with you is what I cherish,
without you I would totally perish.
Intimacy of relationship is what we share,
Togetherness is what has brought us here.
So my love lets enjoy and sing the song
We have travelled far and we will travel long......"

I opened my eyes and thought, was it true?
Such things happen with really few.
I was sitting alone and was forced to think,
Everything I heard and felt was gone with a blink?
I glanced at water and saw around,
In flowing water there was a murmuring sound,
I too started to sing the rivers song,
We have travelled far and we will travel long...

6. "The Creator and The Created"

God is the Creator, we are created,
We are His ultimate desires, much awaited.
Every creating has a meaning,
Take for instance a sun set in evening.
It tells us how lovely His creation is
Sinking like a gull in the ocean.
Mountains inspire us to be bold,
To live for the vision we hold.
Joy and sadness are two phases,
Same as a storm and clear sky cases.
Even a stone preaches us to live life,
Else life to us will act as a knife.
Rose with many thorns tell us,
There aren't many days of happiness,
As many as we spend in sadness.
There are many more to tell
But there goes my school bell
Even this has a story to tell
Similarly God is ringing a bell (calling us)

and saying:
"Bring a Change on This Earth which is a real Hell"

7. "Nostalgic All the way"

At times I wonder what memories are all about,
As I started brooding over this, I uttered a shout.

I realized memories are to feel the presence of past in
present, the time never goes,
Feel the warmth of love, care and fights with friends and
foes.
I decided to lie on a couch, close my eyes and re-live the
day's bygone,
The moments of togetherness, the moments of love
which was not shown.
In flashback times I went, with memories flooding the
view,
Every stage of life eloped totally afresh and just as new.

Memories of childhood with tiny tots called friends
around,
Hot summers, shadows of trees and those chirping
sounds.
Childhood days memories were flooded with innocence,

Tension free attitude, no worry of worldly affairs and no
nonsense.

Energetic and full of life were memories of school and
college days,
Fun and frolic, teasing and pleasing and all other idiotic
ways.
Falling for and Saying "I Love You" to every damsel who
passed by,
and no courage to utter a word to the one on whom we
really had an eye.
"Coward" "Coward" from friends is what filled the
atmosphere around,
standing there like a dumbo with closed eyes and
spellbound.
Teasing by friends on such issues and calling names....
Alas! What the heck has life become we have no time
now for such games.

Late night studies with exams close, with books and
discussions around,
Waiting for midnight to disturb those sleeping by all
sorts of frightful sounds.
Dancing and singing in one time College fests,
enjoyment is all what I see,
As I recollected such small incidents, just then a knock at
door disturbed me.

As I opened my eyes, I was forced to wonder Oh My.....
I could write a thesis on memories of those golden days
gone by.
Why are human being Nostalgic all the way (throughout
life)....?
But then it's good old times that have the final say...
It's more mesmerizing to feel the moments with closed
eyes
Memories are symbolism of everlasting and unbroken
close ties.

So here's to the journey, with all its twists and bends,
For memories are the compass, guiding until the end.
And though we stride forward, with each step and sway,
The essence of those golden days forever shall stay.

8. "Amble in the woods....."

Early morning as I walked past the woods,
Calm and serene ambience, made be brood.

The gentle whispering of the trees could be heard,
Dewdrops on ferns and petals, chirping of birds,
All transit me into the world, different and strange,
The thought process within went far from range.

Visualizing the ravishing Sun with all its cosmic
embrace,
Peeping though the mighty trees with exotic beauty and
grace,
I was standing there spellbound in a state of cogitation,
Mystic nature led me to analyse the beauty with
cognition.

Just then a hiss in the green grass caught my attention,
A squirrel crossed by in all hustle as if in great tension,
Squirrels haste is like a life of a common man and his
needs,

Who ambulates throughout the day to make both ends
meet.

Path ahead was full of leaves, yellow and green.
Adding to the beauty of dawn totally unseen.
The gentle sounds of rustling leaves, caused by gentle
breeze,
Wafting out nature's symphony as soft wind blew by the
trees.

As cool breeze swapped the dry leaves, it seemed to say,
"Come on my friend it's not here for you to stay,
This place is not your destination for today,
Blow with me (Move with me), I will show you the way"

As I was startled by these acts in the vicinity,
I wondered and wondered what is to be done to ignite
the capability?
Realization was, we humans too should not stop at one
destination,
Should keep growing and moving ahead in life with
great perspiration,

Ahha!!! This amble in woods proved to be a journey
fruitful,
Unintentionally I happened to learn lessons in ambience
peaceful.

So I paused for a heartbeat, to drink in the scene,
As if nature itself spoke in whispers serene.
"Life's rhythm is timeless, a dance on the breeze,
Keep your spirit unbound, let your worries find ease."

Thus, I gathered the strength, from each tender insight,
Ready to face the world, with the dawns gentle light.
For in this grand tapestry, woven with love,
I found a connection, a push from above.

9. "Saunter in the clouds"

Flying above the clouds was an exhilarating experience,
Boosting my thoughtful mind into a state of percipience.
The scenic beauty with blue sky and patches white,
Sea of clouds beneath was giving a wonderful sight.

I asked my co-traveller for pen and paper in this high
tech world,
He mocked saying "What is that mobile for? Which you
hold.
To use the option of Notes in my mobile I was told,
Pouring imagination and words were which I could not
hold.

As we flew high the view of ground started to dampen.
Never even my wildest dreams ever I thought this would
happen,
Journey in the sky would take me to a unique world in
air,
Mind surrendering to the imagination which I longed to
share

Clouds carving images of different stature and fashion,
A glimpse of White floating castle also caught my
attention.
The mighty castle which gradually faded away as it
moved ahead,
Merging into the white snow like sheet which was
widely spread.

Another cloud gave an appearance of a hungry lion
roaring,
Sideways floating clouds appeared as if the small animals
running.
Running to save their lives and scattering far and wide,
Mingling into the coming clouds as if found a place to
hide.

Cluster of clouds gave an impression of a beautiful
steeple.
Surrounded by shapes of faces like an assemblage of
people.
Masses busy in some sort of unending serious
discussions,
As if a slight move from position would have grave
repercussions.

A flock of white ducklings swam with their head held
high,
A swarm of black bee like clouds were hovering ready to
cry.
As they engulfed the birds, showers of rain started to
pour,
And the colossal white land turned into a misty black
floor.

The black cloud army on the territory so impudently
intrigued,
White army was totally unarmed and got easily fatigued.
Just then from nowhere other soldiers dressed in white
entered,
And the invincible black brigade was attacked and
centred.

Shaken was I with the pilot's announcement of time to
land,
My eyes peeped into the time on the mobile in my hand.
I wondered how I was carried away by the candescent
state,
Returning to the actual moment was what I really hate.

I wondered Why? Why was I carried by such a spate of
thoughts?

Were other passengers like me in such contemplation
caught?
In silent ambience as I rolled my eyes to see around,
A totally different scenario and moment was what I
found.

I wondered life is also full of such incidents big and
small,
Taken by some beautiful and some distracting moments
is all,
Either they break us or they make us but life doesn't
stop.
It's all about living in those moments and our solitary
thoughts.

Mingled with wisdom and incommensurable
imagination.
This saunter in the clouds was an indescribable
erudition.

So, as wheels touched the ground and reality snapped
back,
carried the clouds with me, their beauty, a sacred track.
For every ascent must have its descent, every joy finds
its cost,
But in the journey of thoughts, no vision is ever lost.

10. "Unstinting Romance"

As I followed my weekend routine of going to Sai
Temple,
Nothing was new in the day, but still there was one
example.
From the foyer, an old man in wheelchair entered the
Hall,
His Better half was pushing it with all her might
avoiding the fall.

Placing the wheel chair in the middle of The Holy Abode.
She moved forward to pay homage to the Almighty God.
She returned only to find her husband in deep devotion,
She decided not to disturb him and stood in a state of
commotion.

In sanctity she put the Tilak –"The Eye of intuition" on
his forehead,
I read her eyes and they seem to utter some hope and
still look dead.

As if saying, we have walked this far, walking hand in
hand my sweetheart.
May the almighty give us strength to be always together
till death falls us apart.

Love, care and respect with every little gesture seem to
be increased,
Garlanding him in respectful deference with garland
given by the priest.
As if remembering the vow of marriage that she
promised to keep,
"I am and will always be there for you till I go for the
final sleep".

The inciting positive vibes from these love birds filled the
air
Peeling off the Prasad banana she sat beside his wheel
chair,
She gave it to him in parts and he ate like a kid in life's
edentulous stage,
Sitting she hymned her love for God, noticing she wiped
off his dirty face.

They swept out of the Wattled hall with such a solace on
their face,
The love still existed, had grown better and strong at
life's this phase.

What a respite it was for them hymning to the grace of
lord,
The time they had spent together I am sure they both
adored.

Her patience, the care in her expressions and her love
had no price.
I almost never cry, but this eternal love brought tears to
my eyes
While this required introspection and my heart
convulsed to really speak,
I lifted my hands to wipe off those drops seeping down
my cheeks.
.
Seeing their unconditional love tears again rolled down
my eyes,
They were bound to each other with everlasting
unbroken ties.
Their world full of love and care with no place for hate
It's truly said "True love never expires it's beyond
expiration date".

In that fleeting moment, I vowed to cherish each breath,
To weave every encounter with threads of love, defying
death.
For in their embrace, I found lessons profound and clear,

That love casts shadows away, turning despair into
cheer.

As they glided through the doors, stepping into the light,
I realized the true essence of life is this heartfelt insight.
Their journey, a testament that love's light always shines
bright,
In a world where darkness looms, they became the
guiding sight.

With each passing moment, they crafted a legacy of
grace,
A gentle reminder to all, love's the ultimate embrace.
So here's to those who love fiercely, come what may,
For in the tapestry of life, love is the thread that will
stay.

11. "Its SHE!!!! ......but Will SHE be...???"

Once while browsing through TV News Channels,
I was surprised to see discussions going on with expert panels
Discussions on topics prevailing in this pitiful society,
Arguments and suggestions on how to nip them in bud with all anxiety

Coming across a discussion on female foeticide, my eyes could just not blink
How heinous is the act of mankind I was forced to think.
It's just not about the decision of a family, a husband or a wife,
The question is are we so blessed to be decisive on putting an end to a life?

Though gender equality is talk of the town,
Girl in a womb or girl born is welcomed with a frown.
Eloping thoughts lead me to the women around,
Is this something which no one ever found?

Proud we feel celebrating Mother's Day and Women's
Day,
Anxiously we wait whole year for the Rakshabandhan
day,
Looking for girls to be our better half through thick and
thin,
All applaud the women behind every successful man and
kin.

We all look up to the first women (Our mothers) in our
life,
We love sharing our joys and sorrows with our wife.
We cherish childhood days of fights with our sisters,
Still few of us don't want a girl child on our lifes
registers.

What an irony of the hypocrisy of our thoughts,
Where are we heading for with such a lot,
But is this exactly what we need to find?
Many thoughts started crossing my mind.

The Challenge is comprehensive addressal of all aspects,
The girl who comes into this world should live with
respect.
As I further browsed the channels my thoughts sailed
And the perplexed state of my mind still prevailed,

Is this world safe for the girl to be here?
Do we as humans have nothing to fear?
Struggling with thoughts as of now,
I just wondered why and I wondered how?

We talk of liberation and dreams of future bright,
Yet the hope of a girl child is extinguished from sight.
Each statistic alarms, but still, we persist,
Turning blind to the reality that we cannot resist.

So let's unveil the truth, let's shatter this guise,
For every girl deserves to rise and realize.
Let compassion reshape the lens of our view,
And cultivate a world where each girl can bloom anew .

12. "Tree's Last Agony"

I was strolling past a nature park in vicinity of my home,
With head held high in high spirits as I continued to
roam.
Awe stuck was I by, "A Bleeding Tree", an artful creation.
The serene beauty and the sight instilled sense of elation,

The wooden sculpture of a bleeding tree with a child in
arms.
A Mother cuddling her baby to the lullaby's with
charms,
The view was captivating; two men were axing its trunk
Blood red axe and the motherly embrace more shrunk.

I wondered why? Why this depiction has arrested my
attention?
Standing there as I tried to envision the bone of
contention.
I sensed the child asking his mother" Oh MA! What is
happening?

Though being axed no sign of fear, no pain and still you
battling.

Smilingly she said," Baby this is on from centuries and
not new,
We have been axed, burnt and uprooted this way by few.
We have been their support and help whenever needed,
This gesture without appreciation has always been
unheeded".

The baby said'" MA but I wanted to live and grow
How can I communicate this to them or How do I
show?"
The mother still smilingly replied, "It's just not worth",
Just be happy as we both are together as we are
unearthed.

As I came out from this state of unbridled ecstasy,
I longed to continue to live in the world of fantasy
Where I could listen to the things, which generally go
unheard.
The reflection of truth, now lucid which once was
blurred.

I wondered about the pitiful state of the human race,
How they love, adore and exploit for their own grace

I was forced to think how truly trees feel and suffer
silently,
Not so blessed to raise hue and cry and response so
violently.

The only noise they raise is with air while felling to the
ground,
Which fills the atmosphere sending a message all
around.
"At hands of so inhuman humans I fall down with all my
might,
Proudly living for others throughout my life I meet this
plight."

It offers fruit to eat, wood for home, restrain from sun
and rain,
A small gesture of care is better than repentance and
pain.
Let us as humans show some contrition for this heinous
crime,
Make "Plant a Tree" rather than axing as our motive
prime.

This is a plea to all; even Plants can feel the pain and
affection,
Let's live together as benefactors with complete
perfection.

We are endangering our own existence by destroying the
trees.
"SAVE TREES to LIVE", and feel the breath giving breeze.

13. "Exhilarating Experience in the Museum"

Museum as a place of rare things was opinionated since I
was a child,
A movie "Night in the Museum" had made the
imaginations wild.
With age as time elapsed and the thinking mind grew.
I longed for visiting a museum to see something old with
learning new.

As I stepped inside the colossal building the galleries
were large and wide.
With historical depictions in form of painting and
statues on all sides
Walking through different galleries I was spell bound
and wondered
To the beauty of artefacts and rare collections I
completely surrendered.

My mind completely lost in the unknown world of
history,

Lost in the rarity of items depicted and their unfolding
mystery.
What a life? What an art? What a talent? What
collections?
Wow! Wow! Oh My God! were the only recurring
expressions.

With the rich holdings stored every gallery or space had
a different story to tell
Moving through the decorative arts gallery, I was
flabbergasted as if under a spell
I wondered why? Why Am I here, Is there something to
experience, learn and share,
Just then a strange co-relation between a museum and
life struck my mind from nowhere.

The family values and rich cultural traditions are what
our elders share
Museums store the rich heritage through artefacts,
paintings and collections rare,
An unmatched blend of past with present and
amalgamation of future, in same fashion
As an individual the need is to carry forward the legacy
of our culture and traditions,

In life the mode of handover and storage is different if
rightly analyzed,

But similarity of saving it for future generations to come
is to be apprised.
Just then a bronze statue of a dancing girl caught my
attention,
Dance to the tune of life and keep enjoying is a special
mention.

Her poised grace dancing whispers tales of joy, struggle,
and heart's intention.
In each twist and turn, the rhythm of time could be felt,
a cosmic connection,
Echoes of laughter, tears, and triumphs in every curve of
her form,
A reminder that life, like art, is an endless journey, a
transformative storm.

I stood mesmerized, as if the world outside had ceased to
exist,
Lost within the echoes of history, I couldn't help but
persist,
To ponder over the frail yet fierce memories that bind us
together,
In the tapestry of time, woven with threads of our shared
endeavor.

Each artefact a whisper of its time, a lesson in
evolution's flow,

Inviting us to reflect on where we've been, and the seeds
we sow.
As I turned to leave, the museum lingered, etched deep
in my soul's core,
A sanctuary of stories, a compass guiding us to explore

14. "A Killer Guerdon"

At times thinking about the golden days of my
childhood,
I go into a deep thought whether the technology is so
good.
Blessed I feel to be born in the days of no technology,
Days of total different methodology and different
psychology.

Children playing in neighbourhood and playgrounds,
With quarrels and cheerful faces all around.
Creating ruckus playing around in neighbourhood.
Today's children are missing this glorious childhood.

Games of hide and seek, where finding the person was a
target,
Today kids are finding someone animated to kill on
internet.
Games of *"pithu"*, *"chor sipahi"* *"langdi taang"* & *"stapu"*
In today's so called modern scenario these all seem to be
taboo.

Surprises are lost in the vicinity of social networking,
From close relations and facts we have started shirking.
Social sites updates are all that we do and we stalk,
Facebook and WhatsApp messages is all how we talk.

People had time for one another, time to interact &
listen,
Addiction to updates on social sites has left us in
isolation.
A state of isolation which we do not notice or feel,
Questioning our very existence and something from us it
steals.

Many friends , known and unknown, none around when
you alone.
Our whole world is the web world and applications in
the phone.
Update the status as "enjoying or getting bored", "happy
or sad",
They see, comment, ignore or like it, which is the
concern they had.

I really wonder and wonder why technology was born,
Why everyone is so stuck to it like a leech and a worm.
Instead of mastering our own baby we have become
slaves to it,

More awareness, less interaction and addicted to it every
bit.

Let technology take a backseat in life's journey,
Team up with it than living in the world of tyranny.
Technology is a current helping life's ship to sail ashore,
Never forget the ones who are aboard and need you
more.

So pause a moment, breathe in nostalgia's sweet air,
Reconnect with laughter, let memories lay bare.
For every click and swipe, there's a life yet to behold ,
In the embrace of presence, let true warmth unfold.

Let's face the music and take a bow,
Take out some time for our loved ones somehow.
Tech world is something we need to be with and
compete,
But beloved are the one who make us complete.

So raise a toast to moments that light up our days,
In the dance of the now, let our spirits ablaze.
For while screens may connect us, it's love that will
guide,
Embrace one another, let the real joys collide.

15. "Survival of the Race"

Axing the mighty trees for widening of roads
Spoiling the green fields for making abodes.
Seeking Green lush parks in vicinity of our homes.
Isn't it such a pitiful state in what we roam?

For parking our vehicles on roadside tree shade is what
we seek,
Doesn't this hypocrisy require an honest and thorough
sneak?
In the name of infrastructure development where are we
heading?
Destroying our rich beautified heritage and then later
repenting.

With every axe that swings, a promise we abandon,
In the echoes of silence, our future grows barren.
Oh, to cherish the roots, the branches, the leaves,
Is a legacy worth keeping, not one that deceive.

Yet, we pave over nature for a fleeting moment's gain,

Forgetting the whispers of winds, the soft patter of rain.
Chasing concrete dreams as the ecosystems fade,
How long will we march in this relentless parade?

Are Buildings and roads through what our next
generations will breathe?
Planting more and more trees is present scenarios die
hard need.
It's just a heartfelt effort and an initiative that is desired,
Nothing is greater than this respite if this is transpired.

Each sapling planted is a symbol of hope,
In a world wearing thin, struggling to cope.
Let's weave our progress with threads of green hue,
For in nurturing nature, we nurture us too.

So let us unite for a cause pure and bright,
To honor our planet and bring back its light.
With every conscious choice, a path we create,
Towards a future where humanity resonates with fate.

Development in today's scenarios is a dire need,
But at the same time it's a very workable plead,
If we axe one, we should plant at least five,
That's how "To be beatified- Human race" will survive.

16. "Don't Talk to Strangers!!!!! How true?"

Inhibitions of meeting a stranger deluged me,
Perplexed state of mind at the same time confused me.
Step forward or step backward? As curiosity pushed me further,
Still don't know why, but we decided to meet each other.

Though only short and few conversations we had,
Something was binding us as we went ahead.
More interactions followed with talks not finding an end,
We conversed as if we were good old friends,

That rationale and those fears of meeting an unknown,
Like soap bubbles flew and were totally blown.
Spending time together was something we cherished,
That is how our life with each other flourished.

In the dance of fate, where shadows entwined,
We forged a connection, in silence defined.

With laughter as our compass, we roamed through the
night,
Every word a lantern, casting warmth and light.

I wonder and wonder how it happened?
Recapitulating the instances I reckoned.
"Don't talk to strangers", is always not the best,
At times you do have to put yourself to test.

And now I ponder, as seasons unfold,
This friendship's a treasure, more precious than gold.
For strangers once lost have a bond to defend,
In the fabric of life, we've stitched every mend.

As my wandering mind, still in state of rumination,
Roving far and wide uttered in wild acclamation,
It was a momentary idea of meeting which became
fruitful,
Ending the constraints, the fears and making me hopeful.

It was about a decision to meet and listening to my
heart,
This gave our blooming friendship a good start.
I was bestowed with a reliable friend for lifetime,
Whatever the situation, he is always a friend of mine.

So cheers to the moments that led us to this,

A journey of courage, a beautiful bliss.
Embracing the unknown with hearts open wide,
In the dance of two souls, forever allied.

So together we'll wander, through storms and through
gales,
With courage our compass, we'll chart new trails.
n this journey of friendship, let's never lose sight,
Of the magic that sparked, in that first chance of light.

17. "LOVE-The Song of Life"

Happened to talk to a friend who had a failed
relationship,
Distressed he was thinking about those days of
courtship.
As he peeked through the bygone days, heard him say
this
Rightly said "Love is a beautiful feeling", Aye it is,

Two people committed to each other,
Love is in the air and there is no bother.
Pleased to be designated as "Love Birds"
Countless thoughts unsaid, still heard.

Long talks, those vows of staying together,
Flocking like birds of same feather.
Missing each other every nanosecond of a day,
With captivating and soothing words, they play.

Love blooms out of a growing youth,
Everything is new, happy, and smooth.

The lyrics of songs are meaningful and heartfelt,
Sharing situational songs is how things are dealt.

Now as I see the couples moving around,
I wonder what keeps them so bound.
Two love birds live in the world of pretence,
Masked by goodness giving every moment a false
credence.

Initially to impress each other both pretend,
Goodness in everything is how the time is spent.
Million-dollar question is how long does it last?
It finally leaves the two birds in aghast.

The mask of goodness is bound to shed,
Gone out of mind and out of head.
It lasts till one doesn't show his real self,
No one can ever come to your help.

True love is an illusion, Love has lost its worth,
Usage of "Love You" is not in dearth,
Said to every third person we get attracted to,
Fearing saying it to someone whom we really want to.

LOVE is a splendiferous four-letter word,
Just for "someone special" to be heard.
Feel it from depth of heart and be truthful,

Hypocrisy of actions is not at all fruitful.

For the beauty of love lies not in the show,
But in simple moments, shared highs, and the low.
Through storms they may weather, hand in hand they stand,
In realms of emotion, they learn to withstand.

Not everyone in this bitter world is true.
Value the person who loves and cares for you,
Precious and rare are people with beautiful hearts,
Catch hold of them and never ever let them be apart.

So cherish the bonds that are free from despair,
In honesty's glow, let affection declare.
Finding solace in souls that are faithful and true,
Is the essence of love, the rarest of views.

18. "Felo-de-se"

Heard shocking news of suicide of a 25 year old actress,
Were the issues and circumstances for her so tactless?
Why are we led astray by small problems in life's
journey?
How can death emerge a winner when engaged in a
tourney?

I wonder is this also endowed on human by the
Almighty,
The empowerment for committing an act so flighty.
How can so easily we decide in putting an end to this gift
of life?
When we cry loud and panic even for the small cut by
knife.

I wonder about the perplexed state of mind and all I
could reckon,
Powerlessness revealed by an inability to act and the
death it beckons.

Negativity is all that engulfs the moment with no
positive thoughts,
I am sure this is not exactly how the life's battle is
fought.

I wonder are we so weak within or is it that things reach
height,
Making a person totally unable to continue the fight,
It's not easy to brutally kill one self, take poison or get
hanged,
Such atrocity is something which cannot be planned.

It's a heinous act committed out of despair and lost hope,
Hopelessness, depression, social isolation which are not
easy to cope.
Stress factors, mental disorders, fear of failure are no less
to contribute
Financial difficulties, torn relationships may also at times
attribute.

I started wondering why I am giving these things a
thought,
What is that to be highlighted and from these to be
sought
Just then green grass on lawn outside my house caught
my sight,
It's not always about the pitiful plight.

Whatever the take still a person should try to play the
card
Death is no solution; Life is worth living no matter how
hard
Terminating this beauty does not put an end to the
hardships,
It only imputes to make it hard for relationships.

Felo-de se: Is an Act of deliberate self-destruction
*Poem written on 10 June'2013 hearing suicide of Jiah
Khan a Bollywood actress

19. "Cherishing The Human Connections"

I wonder today for how many "Family is an asset", holds
true,
Single Family culture fashion in the cities, is engulfing
the small towns too.

Gone are the days when joint family was considered an
asset
With values of generosity, forgiveness, flexibility and
respect,
In today's scenario is its importance understood even by
few,
Being alone and self-dependent with no liabilities is in
fashion and new.

Togetherness in deeds and thoughts,
With always someone there to share with no empty
slots,
Everyone talking, sharing and at times getting hot
(argumentative)

Then again cooling off with no permanent spots.

A Joint family is just not always about saying that we
love and care,
It's about having someone as strength and being there
(when needed the most),
Realization of this fact came to me after being away from
home for all these years,
There was someone to be with me and for me whenever I
had some fears.

Yet, in this age of haste, we often drift apart,
But the heart knows the way, to the bonds that never
depart.
While the world may shift, and trends may arise,
The essence of family is where true wealth lies.

It's all about cherishing the human connections,
be it a family a friend ,what is required is affection.
Togetherness is an important gradient of family life,
Family is a strength and weakness almost alike.

Proudly I held my head high, to be born and brought up
in joint family,
Sincere thanks to all for inculcating the values which
made me finally.

Apologies for my behaviour which at times made you
disheartened,
Truly I long to go back to the place to be with you all
and be re-enlightened.

So here's to the laughter that echoes through time,
To shared dreams and secrets, to stories sublime.
In this journey of life, we find strength anew,
In the heart of our family, together we grew

So let us gather, let us heal and repair,
In the laughter we share, our burdens we share.
For each moment spent together, is a thread of gold,
A tapestry of love that never grows old

20. "Seclusion... A Moaning Thought"

As I woke up in the vicinity of night, struggling with my
sleepy eyes
Glimpsing at the ticking wall clock I wondered how the
time flies.
Something I could hear, and hear it loud, which drew my
attention,
held me back tied to bed, silently, fearing which I cannot
mention

Aah!! It was a stray dog crying in the vicinity of night,
Oh my! I somehow pity the poor animals plight,
As my thoughts took an unknown flight.
I started wondering with an insight.

As per our mythology it's related to seeing "God of
Death",
Moaning of dogs is related to someone's ending breath.
But does it really hold true, or is it just a common view,
With wide open wings as always my thoughts flew.

Why doesn't the dog moan during broad day light?
Is it the fear of darkness of the night?
In the dark hours when no one is visible around,
Is it the desolation it feels, reflected in the moaning
sound?

In seclusion we too weep about our actions unheard,
We get insight of our own self which is quite absurd.
We analyse and conclude about the world around,
It's the time when many new things are found.

This contemplation is a pleasant reverie like being on a
cliff,
Every human being fears the darkness (loneliness) no
matter how stiff.
A person pretending to enjoy the loneliness is whenever
testified,
Given a chance will cry loud as loneliness is never
justified.

Loneliness of heart, and seclusion of mind, Is just one of
its kind
Like the dog, humans too cannot fight and solace they
need to find,
Solitary life is not worth a life is the truth we need to
confide,

Feelings are something which even the stray dog could
not hide.

Life is all about togetherness and more than just to be
survived,
It's about living it to the fullest and living it with pride,
It's about being with someone, whom you adore,
It's about a family, a friend, a tie and about much more.

"Companionability" was the realization which was to be
understood,
I slowly crept into the bed with nothing more to brood.

As dawn approached, I pondered deeply, turning in my
head,
The gentle touch of sunlight, breaking the cycle of
dread.
Through the sorrow and pain, amidst the silent strife,
What truly matters is the love that gives us life.

21. "Mysterious Beauty of Eyes"

A melodious voice caught my attention,
I turned around with great passion.
I saw a girl; her hidden face sent a positive vibe,
Wonder stuck I stood there as a honey bee in bee hive.

She talked and laughed, but her looks still a curiosity,
Knowing her more was now the necessity.
As she turned around, I was spell bound,
Blue eyed damsel with killing eyes was what I found.

Her face was all covered, and her eyes shown bright,
May be it was to keep the spirit of broad daylight.
Her eyes spoke a language of love and beauty,
I couldn't resist and appreciating it was my duty.

I wondered for the beauty in her eyes totally speechless.
Innocuous expressions of rotating balls were priceless.
The exotic eyes made the silence more eloquent,
The ambience was so serene, calm and elegant.

My attention fixated on eyes as though by a spell,
The type of my cognitive condition, I cannot tell.
So much that her elope from the place was totally
unheeded,
The moment passed and consciousness was what I
needed.

In that moment frozen, where time seemed to cease,
Her gaze whispered secrets, granting my heart peace.
A fleeting glance felt like an eternal embrace,
In the tapestry of life, she wove my heart's lace

I wondered and realized about the real mystery
and somehow I wondered about the chemistry.
The chemistry of eyes, the word unspoken beautifully.
The cogitations were recorded in the mind dutifully.

Returning from the pensiveness, exquisite thoughts I
hold.
About expressions, elegance which were all too bold.
Eyes which were lavishly elegant and refined.
Mysterious beauty which cannot be easily defined.

For the beauty of moments can linger and grow,
In a world painted with dreams, where heartbeats flow.
I'll cherish her image, as days turn to years,

A timeless connection, beyond laughter and tears.